Ransom Reading Stars

Sky Dive
by Stephen Rickard

Published by Ransom Publishing Ltd.
Unit 7, Brocklands Farm, West Meon, Hampshire GU32 1JN, UK
www.ransom.co.uk

ISBN   978 178591 841 4
First published in 2010
This revised edition published 2019
Reprinted 2023, 2024

Copyright © 2019 Ransom Publishing Ltd.
Text copyright © 2019 Ransom Publishing Ltd.
All photographs copyright © 2008 Red Devils. All photographs taken by L/Cpl Steve Candlish, Team Cameraman, Red Devils. Many thanks to Steve for all his help.

A CIP catalogue record of this book is available from the British Library.

All rights reserved. No part of this publication may be reproduced, stored in a retrieval system, or transmitted, in any form or by any means, electronic, mechanical, photocopying, recording or otherwise, without the prior permission of the publishers.

The right of Stephen Rickard to be identified as the author of this Work has been asserted by him in accordance with sections 77 and 78 of the Copyright, Design and Patents Act 1988.

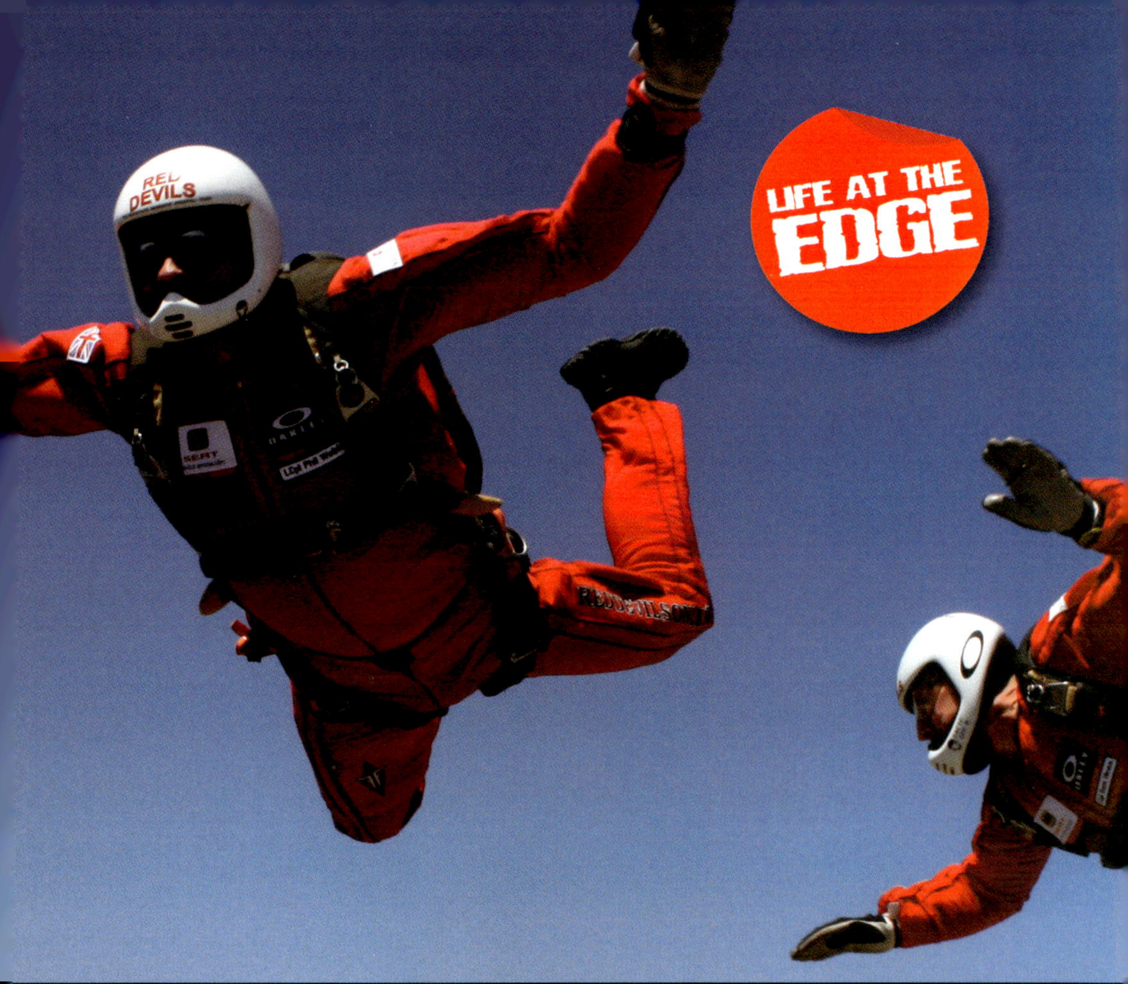

SKY DIVE

LIFE AT THE EDGE

Stephen Rickard

Main parachute.

Helmet.

Jump suit.

Yellow toggle.
In an emergency, the sky diver can pull this toggle to cut away the main parachute.

Altimeter.
This tells the sky diver how high he is.

The Red Devils

The Red Devils parachute display team are part of the British Army.

Sunglasses.
To protect the sky diver's eyes.

Knife.
In case the sky diver gets tangled up in his parachute.

Flag.

Sky Dive Data

Jump height: 13,000 feet
Free-fall time: One minute
Parachutes: Two. (One is a spare, just in case!)
Top speed: 193 km/hour (120 mph)

Hi! I am a sky diver.

I am in the Red Devils parachute team.

That's my job.

We put on parachute displays for people to see.

We jump from an aeroplane and the crowds watch us as we fall.

This is sky diving.

For the first part of the jump, we do not open our parachutes. This is called "free fall".

When we are in free fall, we can move around in the air. This is part of the display.

We practise our display on the ground.

We call this "dirt diving".

We ride on things like big skateboards.

We call them "creepers". They help us work out what we will do in the air.

The parachute must be packed well. If not, it may not open properly.

So each person packs his own parachute. That way, each person can be sure it was packed carefully.

Now we are in the aeroplane.

It takes us up to a height of 13,000 feet. That's nearly two and a half miles up in the sky.

Now we can jump.

The jump master tells us when we are over the jump site.

If we jump too soon or too late, we might land in the wrong place.

As I jump, I can see the other sky divers in front of me.

Some of us have smoke cans tied to our feet.

They will make smoke trails as we fall. This makes it easier for the people on the ground to see us.

The smoke looks good, too!

Ten seconds later, we are falling at 120 miles per hour.

We fall for about 10,000 feet without opening our parachutes. This is free fall.

This takes about one minute.

As we fall, we move our bodies to link up with each other. It's like swimming in the air.

It is great fun!

But I must keep my focus and make no mistakes. Don't forget – we are falling to the ground at 120 miles per hour.

Now you can see smoke from the smoke cans. This makes a good display for the crowd on the ground.

This part of the sky dive is all fairly safe.

In a sky dive, you don't get hurt in the air.

If you do get hurt, it will be when you hit the ground.

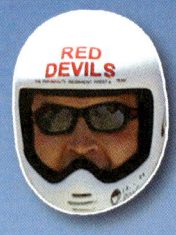

Now we have fallen nearly 10,000 feet. We are about 2,500 feet up in the air. It is time to open my parachute.

If I open it any later, I will be going too fast when I hit the ground.

I pull the toggle and my parachute opens.

We call this "dumping out".

With my parachute open, my speed quickly slows from 120 miles per hour to about 10 mph.

Now we carry on with the next part of our show.

We can pull on our parachutes to move sideways as we fall.

So we can link up and make different shapes.

Now I am coming in to land. We all need to land close together. We call the landing place the drop zone.

When we are on the ground, we pick up our parachutes.

We carry them off the drop zone.

Jargon Buster (word list)

altimeter
chain of death
creepers
diamond
dirt diving
drop zone
dumping out
emergency
free fall
helmet

jump master
jump site
jump suit
parachute
Red Devils
steering lines
sunglasses
toggles
tri by side